EVERYTHING IS A
DEATHLY FLOWER

EVERYTHING IS A DEATHLY FLOWER

POEMS BY

MANEO MOHALE

UHLANGA

2019

First published in Cape Town, South Africa by uHlanga in 2019
UHLANGAPRESS.CO.ZA

Distributed outside South Africa by the African Books Collective
AFRICANBOOKSCOLLECTIVE.COM

ISBN: 978-0-6398108-2-9

Edited by Francine Simon
Cover design and typesetting by Nick Mulgrew
Cover image by Wade Moonsamy and Samu Belle / BCKRDS / BCKRDS.COM
Proofread by Jennifer Jacobs

The body text of this book is set in Garamond Premier Pro 11PT on 15PT

ACKNOWLEDGEMENTS

This book is made and held by many hands.

Thank you to the Coast Salish peoples, especially the xʷməθk-ʷəy̓əm (Musqueam) on whose land I lived for five beautiful and painful years.

Thank you to Nick, for your unwavering faith in me and this little tome, and for your gentleness and patience in this process. Thank you to Fran, for being the best editor I could ask for, for your vulnerability and your incredible eye. Thank you to Genna, for asking me to write.

Thank you to Mama MJ and the Morifi-Winslows for opening up your home. This book's backbone was written on your gorgeous balcony. Ke'a leboha Mme Malitha for endless cups of tea, shy conversation and deep care.

Thank you to Mama Kentse, Ntate Giggs and the Mgeyane family for your son, for your love and support.

Thank you to the writers and artists whose work and words guide, inspire and ignite these pages. Special thanks to Leah Horlick, Mme Makhosazana Xaba, Leah Lakshmi-Piepzna Samarasinha, Prof. Pumla Dineo Gqola, Saeed Jones, Nakhane, Jillian Christmas, Vivek Shraya, Kopano Maroga, Luvuyo Equiano Nwayose, Jane Shi and Kelsey Savage for your light.

Thank you to my teachers, Benita Bunjun, Janet Baylis, Melissa Jane Cook, Vaughn Carlisle, Prof. Michael Zeitlin, Prof. Erin Baines and Dr. Delia Douglas. Thank you to Juliane Okot-Bitek, for your guidance, for white words written on glass. Thank you to Milisuthando Bongela, for every single squeeze.

Thank you to Andi Zeisler and the entire Bitch Media team for publishing my work, and holding space for the essay that gave birth to this book.

Thank you to Ashley Bentley and the amazing people at the Sexual Assault Support Centre. Thank you to Nicole Chanway, for finding the difficult words, and giving them to me.

Thank you to Itumeleng Mamabolo, I couldn't have written this book without your ear.

Thank you to my chosen families, and my loves. To Eric, Gale and Andile, thank you for celebrating every tiny and not-so-tiny moment. To Mike, Chloé, Irving and Mwango, thank you for teaching me, holding me, and not letting go. To Sejal, Roya, and Missy, my sisters. Thank you to PENG, my newest family. Deep, unknowable, unsayable gratitude to K, Keneilwe, Sean, Deyan, Alem, Francis, Kyle, B, Tita and Tito Arevalo, Eli, Dani, Melite, Danni, Dinika, Kalo, Sydney, Vuyi, Fela, Desire, Khanya, Darren, Justin, Gomi, Naeem, Tia, Zoé, Sarah, Kelly and Leigh-Ann, Cicely-Belle, Simón, Titi Naomi, Fatima, and Joshua.

Thank you, Neo.

Thank you Tshepi, Mama, Pa, the Thekisos, Chiotas, and Mashas for your love.

— M.M.

CONTENTS

For Wenzekahle Lesedi Mgeyane

LETSATSI

In your mother's red golf, you ask her what benoni means.
Son of my sorrow – hearing the sun instead,
you turn the word over in your mind like a coin.

Ghosts are living in mine dumps
as your mother drives you home. Honeycomb
mountains are brittle. Tomorrow, you ask

her for a crunchie after school. Like all names
of the bible, benoni sounds ancient. Out
your mother's mouth magic. Manjink. Meijik.

You are still small enough to hide
inside the good book's rice paper pages. You do not know yet,
what you are – have not had leviticus angled at you

like an ice-pick. For now, the bible is a hand drum
for women draped in white and blue. Ko katlehong,
in a pockmarked garage, they are women made of clouds

and ocean. They make terrifying sea-wide music. Sgubhu:
the plastic bottom of everything that has a heart. Shells
and bottletops on ankles. How neatly

old and new gods sit together.
In school, you meet a man named cecil john
and learn the word *pioneer*.

Turn the word over in your mind like a coin.
Your mother is a witness. Your mother is
a pioneer, not yet knocking on doors

to tell people about the good news.
You wonder if cecil was a witness too, wonder
on whose doors he knocked,

for which god, to spread what good news.

I

*Thoughts are like opposing currents meeting.
On paper I wish to write clearly and plainly about the
havoc that has been wreaked on me. I had planned to
say "my body" instead of "me", but at that moment I
realised how all-encompassing that event was.
It is a wide net. It is an ocean and not a river.
It is some unknowable, expansive tundra
and I have nowhere to hide.*

— *Nakhane*, Piggy Boy's Blues

PHALAENOPSIS (MOTH ORCHID)

This orchid is an open mic. Night blooming,
held out to you now as a beginning –
soft-fleshed. Throat opened

in glossed rhythm. Rehearsed
young and memorised.
Back when you were both girls,

she was a poet. Slamming
something against the air
too pretty to be truth.

You listened anyway, confusing
cadence for cotton. Charmed,
you slipped yourself between two brass-noted

nigerian girls in conversation.
Graphite curve of your name
on the line-up, thrice syllabled.

You plan to sing, but you're nervous
how your voice will be harvested
by orientation-week ears. This orchid

is unbloomed and bare. Windowed downstairs
in the university residence hall,
a stolen continent away.

Tiny sesotho seedlings
your mother tucked under
your tongue already withering

so far from home. Waiting
for your turn, you hum Mme
Makeba to keep them warm.

Afterwards, ignoring applause,
you look for her. The un-truthful poet.
She finds you the next day,

on the way to class and gives you the first
of your many titles, with a promise
that blooms darker now:

You're the tiny singer, right?
Sorry I missed you. Don't worry.
I'll catch you later.

CHERRY YAM'

In the blessed dark of freddie wood,
she catches you laughing at chekov.
You're here because you love the theatre,
and you're easily charmed by a cherry tree.

Half rapture/rain dance, you (un)notice
when she thieves your giggles
for her pocket – taking careful note
of what makes you laugh.

                    What is it that makes a ritual?

You are a studded sequence of words
and gestures. Performance
in sequestered space. Tonight,
you are an offering. This ritual is time

feasting on itself –
an exchange and a ceremony.
She loves you after chekov,
and you give her your hand somewhere

between stoppard and beckett. You hide
her hand in your pocket. She is caterpillar-soft.
Tonight, she is only as dangerous
as dreams

and you have loved white lace
all your life, threading
your babybrown fingers
secretly through nkgono's tablecloth.

DIONAEA MUSCIPULA (VENUS FLYTRAP)

I am stuffing her with confession.
She sucks the fat, licks her fingers.
— *Jeanann Verlee*

when you finally meet her appetite // & its attendant inevitable
conditions // feed it the sweet meat // of your favourite song //
seed it in the backseat of a car // lyric by lyric // watch for its pulp
// try not to make a mess // stave off its yearning with memory //
dig your brother's impromptu road trip // out of its soil

place on an enamel plate // serve it at johannesburg summer
temperature // roads still steaming from sudden shower // garnish
memory with jacarandas // the appetite has a taste for the placidly
exotic // now // that its jaws have a taste for the city // give it more
// especially the gold

// placate the appetite // with bite-sized monochromatic histories //
strip struggle heroes of their barbed wire // & thunderous complexity
// so as not to bruise its gums // make your history digestible // you
know exactly what I mean

hold off its desire for marrow // while it picks its teeth // hand it the maw & sinew of your first love // watch it bite at her bottom lip // turn your head at the stain // claws on her pomegranate apologies // fork poking into the boyish pillow of her cheek // fight // off temptation to clean the red river // instead decant your fear

platter the grey-purple // katlehong sky // pebbled grains after rain // your father's camera // your mother's five rings // your sister's effervescent laughter // pay this bounty for your passage // over the bridge between this place // & that place // between home & whole

marvel at your own hands // once it's had its fill // once it finally decides to come home

LOBELIA (TAKE A SEAT)

let the threshold be crossed   let wood turn
to carpet   let night ask its first question
let the silence answer
let the bed be a border   let the bean pretend to sleep

let walls damply ossify   let the blanket bear witness
let night clear its throat   let
silence thicken   let the root take its hold   let it arch
against struggle   let
the threshold be
crossed   let the threshold be crossed   let the threshold be

turn away now
take the bean with you   turn away
something awful is happening

NIGHT JASMINE

we are here	we are leaving
this body is ours	watch us leave this room
this moment is a teacher	a biology lecture hall, emptied
with things to say	seats vacant and talkless
let us dissect it	d i s s o c i a t e
separate stem from stamen	fragmented safely, lifted
separate fingers from flesh	separate stigma from style
watch how her fist blooms now	whose palm is warmer, here?
this is history	this is memory
night jasmine	already wilting
white with nectar	wet

now that we have made this beautiful, do not look away

NEMESIA (WELL, THANK YOU)

The electric spritz of a naartjie, un-segmented
　　its oil suspended like a question mark

　　in the air. You smell it even
　　before you come up the stairs.

The morning after, you find her
sitting cross-legged on the patio.

A cup of rooibos, drained already.
Its elbow angled away from this

　　bright orange carcass

somewhere between the fourth
and fifth step, you decide to pretend.

Her citrused smile confirms it. With
your answer already

sitting on your tongue, she walks the question
to you, on a leash:

　　How did you sleep?

MORAPA-ŠITŠANE

for survivors

dear reader,

are you still there?

take a second, now.

breathe //

with me.

EVERYTHING IS A DEATHLY FLOWER

In place of no, my leaking mouth spills foxgloves.
Trumpets of tongued blossoms litter the locked closet.
Up to my ankles in petals, the hanged gowns close in,
mother multiplied, more – there're always more.

— Saeed Jones

The memory returns to me as a dream.
Inkblot rising black, weeping porous on the night's page.
In place of my room, I lie sleeping in an open forest,
moss a bed beneath me, blanket of cedar leaves – fragrant
and warm as prayer.
Until you arrive. In all your silent menace
you are keeping watch. Your night vigil brief,
searching for a moment when my sleep dips deepest.
You sneak into the moss and touch me without my consent.
In place of no, my leaking mouth spills foxgloves

soundlessly onto the pillowed green.
You do not stop. Instead, you mistake the flood of petals
from my mouth as pleasure. You do not stop. Instead,
you read my body's rigidness as Yes. You read my silence as Permission.
You read my closed eyes as Assent. And my turned head
as Of Course I Am Black and Woman and Queer
What Else Could My Body Be For But Entry
How Else Am I Legible But As Safe To Violate
Everything is a deathly flower.
Trumpets of tongued blossoms litter the locked closet

standing unmoved behind us. Panic paces its itch
across my back and for a moment, I forget my power.
Until I arrive. In the dream, everything is different.
I will my eyes to open. I throw you off of me
onto the floor. I summon the vines to snake
around your wrists like venom. In the dream, the ground
asks you what on earth you are doing.
In the dream, everything rises to protect me.
The petals from my mouth are survivors. I am
up to my ankles in petals, the hanged gowns close in

ensnaring you and suddenly I am safe. Everything
is different in the dream. In the dream, I am safe
forever. I leave my moss bed with bare feet.
Somewhere a lover calls me by name.
"Gift-mother," she says.
We find each other by the water. I
leave the foxgloves behind me.
Every petal that fell
from my mouth is a survivor, they are my
mother multiplied, more – there're always more.

II

Incredulity is a soft-paced
wonder
& in the thick of day
memory is a slippery thing

— Juliane Okot Bitek, "Day 61"

COLOCASIA (DELTA)
after Jeanann Verlee

He is hungry and sweet. He is an open palm,
but she is a jar of flies tonight.
Waiting for the 99, she tells the story

while holding groceries. It is about a striped pole
in the middle of the ocean. It is about
a yellow line, two tongues hiding in a mine dump.

She is a cracked thread spreading
on a windshield. The sound of her mouth is anything
but crystal. He is trying to understand

but the bus is here. He is an open palm
so they walk. She is a green dress unravelling.
This story is a gulping thing, alive.

On the corner of broadway and balaclava he begins
to understand, braces near a bench as it dawns
terrified now, of the water.

When the story finally arrives, everything black
is a river. She is a delta now
un-sedimented and wide, a shuddering category

veined blue with narrative.
No longer an open palm, made sharp
with shock, he wants a reckoning. A case file

yawning open, a court-room brimmed
with judges, a banishing, a punishment.
The water recedes, leaving her grocery bags leaking.

Both of them damp now, forgetting the way home.

GAZANIA (TREASURE FLOWER)

I am looking for the exit. I am looking for my stomach's voice. I am looking for nkgono. I am looking for her twisted root. I am looking for the door above it. I am looking for her iron cross

I am looking for a catholic shoot. I am looking for thick-ankled sky. I am looking for a railway. I am looking for his soapy arm. I am looking for a remedy. I am looking

for the dream. I am looking for it soaked in snakes. I am looking for my blood's message. I am looking for my country's jaw. I am looking for the night mountain

I am looking for her flooding wounds. I am looking for answers. I am looking for my tongue again. I am looking for rancid prophecy. I am looking for revenge. I am looking for a blade now. I am looking for the words

splitting my spine. I am looking for my lovers' teeth. I am looking for their tongues again. I am looking for a seed. I am looking for the lizard in my name. I am looking for betrayal. I am looking for a sterile light. I am looking for the word eating my eye. I am looking for the backwards-river. I am looking for my gender now. I am looking for its burial. I am

looking for the dead. I am looking for the depth-less pool. I am looking baradi baka. I am looking for their yellowed men. I am looking for my fever's birth. I am looking for butha-buthe. I am

looking for blood. I am looking for burnt women. I am looking underneath me. I am looking at the way they left. I am looking for the moaning. I am looking

for a sweeter shame. I am looking for the dogs and why they speak my name in januaries. I am looking for my mother, for the mound and its only reason. I am looking for my sugared mouth

now open again for another.

HELL & PEONIES

Interred in narratives of racism,
we tried to detonate them with counternarratives.
We wait for narrative to do what war should or might do.
— Dionne Brand

1: LENS

an army base on copper ground: a photographer asks an american soldier
to put his head down on a hard table facing sideways   towards the camera's open mouth

    stay still, she says   the photographer fiddles with her 4 x 5   sharpens the steel

light into focus   time is taken   hidden in blue bags of aether staring   at
the lens' dark tongue   the soldier lets down his guard   the   photographer
captures the image   waits for the next soldier
    to lay down

2: APERTURE

a classroom on patina: four years later   hear how the autumn hums
          , your abuser   presents the photographer's work   for an exercise
in transitional justice   each now in your final year
empire is nothing   you are in class together
appears in sleepy procession   but photogenic momentum   soldier   after   soldier
of intimacy and   power pointed   obscured in the visual grammar
                            vulnerability

3: MIRROR

it's so rare that we see soldiers in positions like these, up close.
ceramic and liminal like we are in bed with them

'terribly vulnerable'

a glance goes through you
the photographer calls them

4: BODY

you pass out in a bathroom.
you do not return to class.

5: FOCUS RING

in ink, as it is in rhetoric   war is a metaphor reserved for women, drugs and terror

   mistakenly defanged   invoked on anniversaries of violence   as   if   its   only

danger is on the page   or in the air   spat at us like teeth   war hides in the tendril

   and the blue helmet   under the silken tie   and coded sanction,

  in the shutter and   the shuddering pact   between

the optical   and the chemical   and the mechanical

6: SHUTTER RELEASE

Take this picture with me.

PORTRAIT OF A BEAN
CONTEMPLATING SUICIDE

waiting
for the ferry
from tsawwassen to lekwungen
a loon disappears
pursuing a fish
into the water:

greener than the foot of the sky

BELIEF (FIVE SUNFLOWERS)

for my chosen family

M_____,
stirring a pot of chai.
clove and cinnamon burning
I pull a pebble out my cheek
and tell.
you throw your own at me
: spice & sediment & mortar

_____é,
guilt is a lei
of pale blossoms
yolked in the centre with doubt
the sand remembers, imprinted
by all you've lost
at the ocean. I am
so sorry. Wait for me.

F_____,
I feel you brace
against a portland pine
at the fracture. No longer
two-stepping your path
to me, you believe me
like cloud-copper
like static chord
like music.

I_____,
over facebook,
you put down your pen
for once, mirrored feathers
& blood-warm. three times
like invocation and chant:
I got you
I got you
I got you

M____,
holding a bright sun
in my mouth
singing

LITTLE MONARCH

I finally burn the vinyl that you gave me, posted
　　　across oceans like a simmering letter. I watch
the plastic twist, black-bent like light near the edge
　　　of a singularity. I hate the sleeve –

　　　　　how it mirrors the little monarch glazing
　　　　　　　the cover of your favourite book. The fire
　　　　　is a jewelled feast, more wet splutter than bonfire.
　　　　　　　I am thinking about empire,

how ineffectual
　　　arrows are. How prayer is also gunpowder.
They say that the missionary's body was pierced
　　　on the beach, now drawn by rope across the sand.

　　　　　I wonder at the sound, maybe a child's wired wheels
　　　　　　　on tar. I am thinking about how *untouched island* reveals
　　　　　who touches and who can be touched. I am
　　　　　　　thinking about how bodies like mine are tribes,

but only on paper. I am thinking about
        my own untouching, how I ate my eyes
in the dark and how you unclenched my fist
        like gunpowdered prayer.

                I was a quiet territory, walking.
                        I was a delicious border, inconveniently occupied,
                terra nullius but cuter, brown
                        and boundaried by reservation.

Tonight, I teach my body a solitary music. Salted
        warm as cumin, baptised in silence. My feet
are blooded and swollen with safety. Grateful now,
        for your lesson, crowned in trauma.

CEDAR

Something pulls this poem downwards.
              We don't have much time –
I've left the questions standing
              like reeds.

                                        They won't disturb us.

Something awful, ghostwritten
              in my bones.
This dire ribbon unfurling.
              I do not trust my intentions here.

                                        But here we are.

Plainly: the person sharing your bed
              did something terrible to me
in the night-room. If you listen closely,
              you can still hear my name

                        rattling in their throat like a stone.

        (their skin warms your skin chilled mine
          their lips graze your lips hushed mine
          their feet wrap your feet trapped mine
          their hands pine your hands pinned mine)

                        twin-ventricled,
                  found now at your feet
                        forgive us.
              What a mess we've made.

DAHLIA

Like the cogency of the air
after a thunderstorm! My
qualities appear before me
and overwhelm me, though
I may not put up much
of a fight against them.
   — Franz Kafka

under this light
the pavement breathes.
nothing but fissures in cement,
& the shrubbed conversation of weeds

beneath me. I'm pleased
by my body's ample.
these hips – a brown pendulum.
the very last time we speak,

we meet at kafka café.
the broad scent of coffee,
kafka is peopled with vancouver's
bespectacled offcuts, dressed in black.

I'm unskilled in departure.
after injury, I'd rather leave
the door ajar than evict.
let yourself out.

your parting shot:

they'll leave you too, once they see.
it'll happen again, you know.

(I know)

III

And we said
Evil and then pain of evil
Be trampled underfoot
To ashes and dust...

— *Keorapetse Kgositsile, "Song for Melba"*

DIFAQANE

We have a mulberry tree in our garden (it is not ours).
    It grows on the other side of a white wall. Yawning

its branches over the electric fence that separates us
    from our neighbours, it sheds its black fruit onto the grass.

The morning I came out to my mother,
    all my lovers arrived instead.

I saw her horror rise as she watched them
    claw themselves from my mouth, hands gripping

at my cheeks to squeeze themselves
    into the air. One by one standing at my side

with gemmed eyes,
    and bound breasts and lips like plums.

My mother's eyes like salt-clouds
    scanning the row, searching for jehovah

fruitlessly. That same morning, I stepped into the garden
    with bare feet, plucked the berries from the ground,

crawled and ate the sun-warmed fruit
    until my lips plumped as bruised smudges.

Falling still, finally
    sensing violence in the scattering.

BAROMA 1:26-28

Although   they   knew   God

God

                          gave

                                            them

                          over

(26) Ka baka leo, Modimo o ba neeletse ditakatsong tse dihlong; hobane hara bona basadi ba fetotse mokgwa wa bona wa hlaho ho etsa ka oo e seng wa hlaho. (27) Ka mokgwa o jwalo le bona banna ba lesitse ho etsa le mosadi ka mokgwa wa teng, mme ba tjhesitswe ke ho lakatsana; banna ba etsa manyala le banna ba bang, mme ba amohela ka ho bona moputso o loketseng bolahlehi ba bona. (28) Mme erekaha ba sa ka ba hlokomela ho tseba Modimo, Modimo o ba neeletse moyeng o hlokang kelello, ba tle ba etse tse sa tshwanelang.

                                          God

                            gave

                them

over

to   a   depraved   mind.

CHRYSANTHEMUM (FEGO CAFÉ)

would you like another pot? another
voice another accent another face
another smell another's hands on me
an other

                                        across this table
                          dimples are still there, but
                                        my mother
                          no longer recognises me

they punctuate this face,
full stops before every
staggered breath, brackets behind
each corrugated iron grimace

                                *some black tea, hot milk
                                and honey please* let me
                                crawl back & reverse
                          the marvel of this blooded birth

I'll be a backward pilgrim
up the canal & back
to the first night-room.
you and your sister were born

on only one fallopian tube,
do you know that?
this spectre sits here with us,
followed us on the train,

the plane, the car ride
YVR LHR JHB
pale & shaking
like the flag I want to raise

Mama I give up,
can I give up
let me
give

Mama,
what happens to us
if I say her name?

DIPHYLLEIA GRAYI

Tell me where I can put you down
I've written the sky from midnight to dawn
and carried you all the way 'til morning
And I am tired

           – Kopano Maroga

at second session I hold a glass plate
in my hands – translucent and gold as the goukamma,
ornamental as apology. Its mass reminds me
of my own grief and how it is still too sharp to swallow.
My first therapist is calm and white. She wears green
to taunt me, so I break her plate. Barely blinking, she unwraps
a parcel and offers it to me instead of anger. Sensing how
taxonomy is both sanctum and shield, she gives me
four words for what happened in the night-room.
Tell me where I can put you down

like this, in shards and fragments. Give me
the page that'll bind your sin in ink and amber –
add this to your extended list of reparations. I
intend to collect everything
I am owed. This scarred stomach is testimony
and this grammar is a set of relationships
between structures of language at the eye-level
of every sentence. They will bare witness.
I know what it means to be time's own shattering:
I've written the sky from midnight to dawn

in close pursuit of an exorcism, only to summon
the smoke of my own shame. This shouldn't surprise
me as much, I am writing in english. In
the beginning I hand my therapist
bids to protect you and handfuls
of my own teeth: you knew not what you did;
you were led by the wrist across a border;
you were jealous of the man sleeping
in my heart's watchtower and I deceived you
and carried you all the way 'til morning

into the night-room
with the poison candyfloss of my charm.
Of course it was my fault.
My therapist watches me break
myself with the same calm. I am less fragile
than her goldwater plate, but I break with
the same spectacular sound. I am made
of something more precious than glass. I am
looking for words now,
and I am tired

16 DAYS OF ATAVISM

(or: my therapist asks me for another name, besides victim)

1. fever-vase
2. this kneeling tongue
3. anxious gift and unwilling offering
4. letša
5. boy hiding a girl hiding a boy under a rib
6. mistress
7. both lewatla and lewatle
8. blood-blossomed archive
9. two-hearted country
10. mbokodo's opposite
11. second and last blade
12. grandmother's unstitched scandal
13. tselane
14. a sharper knife than "allegedly"
15. metamour
16. one who carries her lover in her name

GOOGLE TRANSLATE FOR GOGO

DETECT LANGUAGE	SOUTHERN SOTHO (SESOTHO)
~~Grandmother, I'm sorry I've been holding on to this for so long but I want to come out to you, I'm a non-binary demigender pansexual polyamorous queer femme~~	
~~Grandmother remember _____ who came to visit us and stayed in our home and ate our food and played with the little ones she isn't a she anymore, she's a they, they did something awful I am so afraid of saying the word you understand because I don't want to see you shrink I cradle your weak heart and high blood with so much fear~~	
Grandmother, like you, I survived.	Nkgono, joale ka wena, ke phepile kotsi.

ARS POETICA (I)
for Milisuthando

by writing
you text
that I am
transporting ground
fertile enough
to carry the weight
and mass of messages
tune and tune and tune
you can always just open their mouths

you give me back my name
we wait for you
the gift of yours
walking in love like unshadowed horses
healed by this pen
this needle

SANDTON SKYE
for Karabo Mokoena

Privileged to be able to do this, a bought safety.
　　We're running out of bubbles and sushi, still

tender from an afternoon of taste and wet
　　and moan and reach. I'm used to love

on the edge of a cliff, unsurprised to find
　　myself in the tempest heart of another

triangle. Both brown and gasping and drunk –
　　the food's arrived. I find a fig-leaf,

and head downstairs. Unknown to me
　　uBaba has been watching us both. Glint

of a silver star on green felt, I feel my steps
　　quicken despite myself. *Sisi* –

is that a girl with you? The one upstairs?
　　What is it? Do you sleep together?

Are you alone here? Do you need anything?
　　I get off at six, if you girls need me

to come up. I can teach you. Unbuckling
　　his belt, so that I'm sure of his meaning.

Back inside the room, I smell smoke.

ARS POETICA (II)
for Juliane Okot-Bitek

poetry is a crater   poetry is a stalling witness   there are dogs at the door and they won't let
me sleep   every poem is a root both nascent and dying in the ravishing ferment   the   only
part of the plant I want to flower   every poem is touched by the leaden soil   I am
awake to appetite and expectation   I am aware of the boisterous fizzy market   for trauma
the rancid red meat of identity   I was very afraid until you asked: *where are the dogs*
now? what do they sound like when they bark?   Julie I am a witness   Julie   I   am
learning my lines   I will see you at the bench again   after this play is over
and the bones are clean

BROTHER, THUNDER

the last time I visited the psychiatric ward
you gave me two gifts
intricate folded offerings
both made of paper

the first – a make-shift bouquet of white medication-cup flowers
held together at the stems with dirty orange rubber bands
bi-polar blooms
the second – an origami swan
green and mottled

(how different both of these were
from your crease-crumpled letters
full of heartspeak and flying colours
gifted just two years earlier)

we sat at a wooden table
in the colourless common room
as sleepy patients watched the television channels flick past
wrists heavy with the noiselessness of days
you: a leaden laugh and your hands underneath the table
me: a leaden laugh and my hands underneath the table
both scratching at our palms
to try and forget where we were

What colour are your shoes right now?
This is the most beautiful thing I can think of
What colour are your shoes right now?
I hope they are making you happy.

brother, you are both mirror and twin flame
when the white coats peek at your brain scans
they see jazz
when the white folks peek at my brown skin
they see jazz

when the doctors ask you to remember simple sequences
face – velvet – red – daisy – chair
you sense the poetry at the fringes
cup your hands to gather light
and give it back to them, brighter
you are the unholy vessel
speaking your ancestors' songs in mathematics
you draw hip-hop into the air
you heal broken pianos with your pain
no, they cannot understand

you are the thunderclap, brother
waiting for the dust's resolution

the hour you called me *ate* – sister beloved
was when I learned you as *kuya* – brother beloved
we are folded together, you and I.

one day
you will gather your bones
and find me

my arms will wait.

ARS POETICA (III)
for Neo

this poem is
a surprised thing,
pleased to be picked up at 3 a.m.:
a nut and a bolt

how can I make you feel safe?
you come home
kneel at my bed
and ask

LINNAEA BOREALIS (STOCKHOLM)

Draw me
a stunning throughline
filled with triangles.

Gently slide your thumb
over the waxing half-moons
under my eyes.

I've never even been
to sweden, but I know
two things to be true:

1) You hurt me.
2) I miss you.

THE NIGHT-ROOM

Tell me about the femme
with the upended gender
the one on the edge of a trigger
— *Kelsey Savage*

this night asks her to leave, and now she does. this night she wears a shirt and becomes another. this night she eats a mango and forgets. this night she joins a chorus and feels uneasy. this night she finds a bridge and writes *me too*. this night she eats their curry and hides their clothes. this night is doused in beer then in gin. this night she freezes up and lets them rage. this night she kisses them and sleeps unnightmared. this night she doubts decision and builds a box. this night she watches curiosity kill a koolkat. this night she joins the women refusing to dance. this night she reaches nakedly, revels at sound. this night she leaves the current that spits her out. this night the room is empty and made of nectar. this night is withered blossom, now.
is open:

FALSE BUCHU

i
~~don't care~~
~~if you~~
believe me

NOTES

Early versions of some of the poems in this book originally appeared in *Prufrock*, *The Garden Statuary*, *From the Root* and *Jalada*, as well as the 2016 and 2017 editions of the *Sol Plaatje EU Poetry Award Anthology*.

"Cherry Yam'" references Anton Chekov's play *The Cherry Orchard* and gestures towards Tom Stoppard's *Arcadia* and Samuel Beckett's *Waiting for Godot*.

"Dionaea Muscipula (Venus Flytrap)" is after Jeanann Verlee's "Carnivores" from her collection *Racing Hummingbirds*, and takes its epigraph from the same.

"Night Jasmine" is a contrapuntal that draws its inspiration from Safia Elhillo's "yasmeen", published in the July/August 2018 issue of *Poetry*.

"Everything is a Deathly Flower" is a glosa that uses the first four lines of Saeed Jones' "Closet of Red" from his anthology *Prelude to Bruise*. Both of the glosas in this collection are indebted to Amber Dawn's *Where the Words End and My Body Begins*.

"Colocasia (Delta)" owes its form to Jeanann Verlee's "The Telling".

"Hell & Peonies" borrows its title from Kenny Jules Morifi-Winslow. It takes its epigraph from "An *Ars Poetica* from the Blue Clerk" by Dionne Brand, and references the photographic work of Suzanne Opton, from her *Soldier* series.

"Dahlia" takes its epigraph from Franz Kafka's short story, "The Way Home", published in *Metamorphosis and Other Stories*.

"Baroma 1: 26-28" is a found poem that uses verses from the Bible (KJV) in English and Sesotho.

"Diphylleia Grayi" is a glosa that borrows four lines from "disappearing acts #3" by Kopano Maroga. The lines "grammar is a set of relationships / between structures of language at the eye-level / of every sentence" are taken from "two takeaways from today's class on grammar" by K. Ho, with permission.

"16 Days of Atavism" is indebted to Danez Smith's "Alternate Names for Black Boys", found in their collection, *[insert] boy*.

"Sandton Skye" is for Karabo Mokoena, whose boyfriend killed her in April 2017 and set her body alight.

"The Night Room" takes its epigraph from "dysphoria" by Kelsey Savage, originally published on *CarnivalDark*.

The epigraphs to each section are taken from, by order of appearance: *Piggy Boy's Blues* by Nakhane (Blackbird Books); *100 Days* by Juliane Okot Bitek (University of Alberta Press); *If I Could Sing*, the selected poems of Keorapetse Kgositsile (Kwela/Snailpress).

uHlanga

POETRY FOR THE PEOPLE | UHLANGAPRESS.CO.ZA

— ALSO AVAILABLE —

All the Places by Musawenkosi Khanyile

In a Free State and *Foundling's Island* by P.R. Anderson

White Blight by Athena Farrokhzad, translated by Jennifer Hayashida
IN ASSOCIATION WITH ARGOS BOOKS, USA

Zikr by Saaleha Idrees Bamjee

Milk Fever by Megan Ross

Liminal by Douglas Reid Skinner

Collective Amnesia by Koleka Putuma
WINNER OF THE 2018 GLENNA LUSCHEI PRIZE FOR AFRICAN POETRY
CITY PRESS BOOK OF THE YEAR 2017

Thungachi by Francine Simon

Modern Rasputin by Rosa Lyster

Prunings by Helen Moffett
CO-WINNER OF THE 2017 SOUTH AFRICAN LITERARY AWARD FOR POETRY

Questions for the Sea by Stephen Symons
2017 GLENNA LUSCHEI PRIZE FOR AFRICAN POETRY HONOURABLE MENTION

Failing Maths and My Other Crimes by Thabo Jijana
WINNER OF THE 2016 INGRID JONKER PRIZE

Matric Rage by Genna Gardini
COMMENDED FOR THE 2016 INGRID JONKER PRIZE

— AVAILABLE FROM OUR FRIENDS AT CRANE RIVER —

The Mushroom Summer of Skipper Darling by Tony Voss

Voices from Another Room by Stuart Payne

AVAILABLE FROM GOOD BOOKSTORES IN SOUTH AFRICA *&* NAMIBIA
& FROM THE AFRICAN BOOKS COLLECTIVE ELSEWHERE

Printed in the United States
By Bookmasters